To Revise or Not to Revise:
The Essential Guide to Reviewing Somebody Else's Writing

By Angela J. Maniak

Skill-Builders Press
Northport, Maine

TO REVISE OR NOT TO REVISE

Copyright 2005 by Angela J. Maniak

ISBN 0-9629337-2-4
Library of Congress Control Number 2004099239

All rights reserved. No part of this book may be reproduced or transmitted in any form or by any means, electronic or mechanical, including photocopying, recording, or by any information storage and retrieval system, without written permission from the publisher.

Respecting Copyright Law

The author respects your desire and privilege to use the materials in this book and on the CD-ROM for your personal use. In turn, she requests that you respect her right to protect the copyright to her materials. You can do this by respecting the following guidelines.

- Use the CD-ROM to print key points and writing tips. Keep the Copyright notice on the printed page as well as in the electronic file.
- Please do not copy the CD-ROM or send the files electronically to another user.
- Please do not copy, scan, or digitize any pages in the book.

If you would like additional copies of the book or CD-ROM, please contact:
Angela J. Maniak
207-338-0108
www.angelamaniak.com

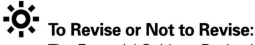

To Revise or Not to Revise:
The Essential Guide to Reviewing Somebody Else's Writing

Dear readers,

To revise or not to revise: that is the editor's dilemma. When a colleague submits a document for your review, is it acceptable to leave well enough alone, or do you want to make the document really shine?

Business and professional managers often act as editors of their work team's writing, and they frequently find themselves caught up in a whirl of revisions, rewrites, and delays. They may find that writers become discontented and procrastinate on their writing assignments. These are costly consequences of a necessary review and editing process.

In this book, I share proven practices that will enable you and your colleagues to break out of a costly review and editing cycle. I show you how to establish a review process that adds measurable value, enhances both the timeliness and quality of documents, and encourages collaboration between writer and reviewer.

By applying the techniques in this book, you will gain measurable payback from the time you invest in reviewing someone else's writing. You will even be able to reduce the amount of time you spend editing and—best of all—see an improvement in writers' skills.

So, put down your pencil and start reading.

Regards,

Angela J. Maniak

TO REVISE OR NOT TO REVISE

TABLE OF CONTENTS

To Revise or Not to Revise:
The Essential Guide to Reviewing Somebody Else's Writing

Table of Contents

Introduction 1

1. Assess Your Own Review Practices 11

2. Identify Your Level of Review 21

3. Identify and Select Your Review Style 37

4. Build a Double-Payback Review Process 51

5. Coach Writers to Write Better 63
   (And Maybe Even Want to Write More)

6. Build Pride of Authorship 83

7. Become a Coach: The Game Plan 97

TO REVISE OR NOT TO REVISE

Notes

Notes

TO REVISE OR NOT TO REVISE

Notes

INTRODUCTION

To Revise or Not to Revise:
The Essential Guide to Reviewing Somebody Else's Writing

By Angela J. Maniak

Wield the Editor's Pencil Proudly (?)

My first professional editing assignment was to edit a series of essays for publication in an academic book. Early on in the process, I received feedback from a writer whose essay I had edited. My boss called me in to tell me an author had commented on my editing, and I was thrilled. I expected to hear compliments on how much I had improved the clarity of the essay and how glad the author was that I had corrected his mistakes.

Much to my dismay, the feedback was quite different. The author had called to complain that "someone was mucking about with my prose." He was offended by some of my changes and felt most of them were unnecessary. I felt chagrined and unjustly accused. After all, I was only helping the author and making his essay better.

If you have ever edited someone else's writing, you may have experienced such a feeling of letdown after returning your revisions to the writer. The author may not have been as grateful or accepting of your changes as you would have liked. Even worse, the writer may have become defensive and given you an even more poorly written document the next time around. You may feel that you are caught in a never-ending cycle of writing and revising, with no relief in sight.

TO REVISE OR NOT TO REVISE

Beware the Trap of the Editing Eddy

Some business documents, after they are drafted by the author, live long lives in an eddy of editing before they ever get to the recipient's in-box. They seem to be trapped, apparently ready to be issued but then back again for another rewrite by the author, an additional edit by a supervisor, or one more correction by an editor.

In the world of business writing, the editing and review process often causes more consternation—and takes more time—than composition itself. Many documents must necessarily be reviewed by the writer's peers and superiors before being approved and distributed. However, this review process often becomes a source of frustration and delay to all the writers and reviewers involved.

How has such a necessary part of the business communication process become so maligned? Why isn't editing seen as the same creative, valuable process as writing? Why are writers and reviewers so often at odds with one another?

In this book, I share proven practices that will enable you and your colleagues to break out of a costly review and editing cycle. I show you how to establish a review process that adds measurable value, enhances both the timeliness and quality of documents, and encourages collaboration between writer and reviewer.

INTRODUCTION

Are You Part of the Editing Chain?

TO REVISE OR NOT TO REVISE

In over 20 years of consulting to professionals on business report writing, I have found the most profound problems to be in the interaction (or lack thereof) between writers and reviewers. Although both parties have the same goal—to publish the best document possible—they often differ in their methods, styles, or attitudes.

Conflict often results, and the consequence is suffered by the organization. Reports get delayed, writing and editing costs escalate, and professionals procrastinate on future writing and editing assignments, fearing that the costly cycle of writing and rewriting will happen all over again.

> **"No passion in the world is equal to the passion to alter someone else's draft."**
>
> — H. G. Wells

Consider "Why?"

Over the years, business writers and editors have posed challenging questions to me repeatedly. Queries I get frequently include the following:

- Why don't accomplished, college-educated professionals write better?

- Why do managers force their personal writing styles on their subordinates?

- Why can't we leave good enough alone?

- Why doesn't my boss (or my subordinate) take a class to improve his own writing skills?

- Why don't writers proofread their own work?

INTRODUCTION

- Why doesn't my boss understand what I have written?

- Why don't we have standard letters, memos, or reports that we can copy?

- Why doesn't my boss show me what she wants in a report so I can write it correctly?

- Why does my writing need to be edited anyway?

- Why do I need to spend so much time editing other people's writing?

All these "Why?" questions suggest to me that neither writers nor reviewers have a very good understanding of the process of writing, let alone the process of collaborating as writer and coach. Instead, writer and reviewer often operate as adversaries, each trying to protect his or her own turf. The process of reviewing someone else's writing becomes the process of revising that writing, and managers act as copy editors, not as coaches.

The professional literature on business writing helps to perpetuate such adversarial practices. Hundreds of books are available on how to write better. Hundreds more are available on how to edit someone else's writing more thoroughly. Precious little guidance is available on how writers and reviewers can become an effective team, producing high-quality, timely documents and learning from each other along the way.

> **"What I have crossed out I didn't like. What I haven't crossed out I'm dissatisfied with."**
>
> **— Cecil B. DeMille,
> a note attached to a rejected script**

TO REVISE OR NOT TO REVISE

☼ Tip #1:

The techniques described in ***To Revise or Not to Revise: The Essential Guide to Reviewing Somebody Else's Writing*** will help you resolve a common problem in the worlds of academic, business, and governmental writing.

On-the-job editing can:

- Escalate the cost of producing documents.

- Delay the publication of important information.

- Demoralize professionals whose written words are rewritten by someone else.

Break Through the Adversarial Editing Cycle

This book intends to break the adversarial editing cycle. It is based on three core principles.

1. No one writes perfectly, and an independent review is a necessary and valuable part of the writing process.

2. The review and editing process can add value only when the reviewer aims for and accomplishes two goals:
    A. Improve the current document, based on established criteria for meeting the readers' needs.
    B. Improve the writer's ability to draft better documents in the future.

3. Writers and reviewers must collaborate to produce high-quality, timely documents at a reasonable cost.

INTRODUCTION

Get Payback from Your Editing Time

If you are a professional who reviews or edits other people's writing, this book will help you accomplish the following goals.

- Get measurable payback from the time you invest in reviewing someone else's writing.

- Reduce the amount of time you spend editing.

- Encourage professionals to write and publish their work results.

- Coach writers to deliver higher quality drafts to you for review.

- Help writers continually improve their writing skills.

- Raise the quality level of documents your work team issues.

- Manage an efficient, cost-effective writing and review process among your work team.

Accomplishing these goals provides a payback to you and your organization because:

- Managerial editing is costly. Each hour you spend reviewing someone's writing adds to the cost of the document.

- Rewriting is rework. A productive and profitable organization cannot afford to have a professional redo the work of a colleague or subordinate.

- Extensive editing is demoralizing to writers, who may continue to turn out poorly written documents.

TO REVISE OR NOT TO REVISE

Do You Get Payback from Your Review Time?

Which Is Greater: The Cost of Your Review Time or the Value of Your Changes?

INTRODUCTION

Who Will Benefit from This Book

If you are a professional or manager who reviews or edits other people's writing as part of your job, this book is for you. I recognize that the word "editor" is probably not in your job title but that, nonetheless, you do have to edit letters, reports, policies, or other documents produced by your work team. The focus of my book is not on the mechanics of editing (where to put a comma, when to change a word), but rather on the process of working with a writer to produce a better document.

Professional copy editors will find value in this book as well, as they learn to look at the writer as well as the document and develop more productive relationships with their writer clients.

Editors of professional journals, newsletters, or compilations will learn how to encourage professionals to submit articles for publication and how to avoid an editorial process that may be discouraging or demeaning to authors.

Tip #2:
Break Through the Adversarial Editing Cycle

You can break through the adversarial editing cycle by embracing three core principles.

1. No one writes perfectly, and an independent review is a necessary and valuable part of the writing process.
2. The review and editing process can add value only when the reviewer aims for and accomplishes two goals:
    A. Improve the current document, based on established criteria for meeting the readers' needs.
    B. Improve the writer's ability to draft better documents in the future.
3. Writers and reviewers must collaborate to produce high-quality, timely documents at a reasonable cost.

TO REVISE OR NOT TO REVISE

Notes

ASSESS YOUR OWN REVIEW PRACTICES

CHAPTER 1

Assess Your Own Review Practices

Key Points

ঽ Editor, Know Thyself

TO REVISE OR NOT TO REVISE

Notes

CHAPTER 1
Assess Your Own Review Practices

Editor, Know Thyself

You will gain the most from this book by assessing and understanding the practices you have already developed in your role as editor or reviewer. To do so, please complete the self-assessment exercises in this chapter. Answer each question candidly, reflecting on the practices you actually use on the job. These are self-assessment exercises: There are no right and wrong answers.

After you complete the exercises in this chapter, read the rest of the book. I will refer back to these exercises along the way and provide interpretation of your responses at appropriate points.

TO REVISE OR NOT TO REVISE

**Exercise #1
Self-Assessment
Reviewing Someone Else's Writing**

Instructions:
Consider that one of your staff members wrote the following paragraph. Review it, making editorial marks as you normally would on the job.

Based on our review and discussion with various personnel, it appears there should be an increased focus on training of employees. Training of new employees and periodic updating is very important to any organization. Also, cross-training employees could be an asset to the organization and many employees will appreciate the opportunity to gain a greater understanding of areas around them. We recommend management take this opportunity to perform a comprehensive and fresh look at the training approach. Additionally, training courses or seminars should be developed for significant changes in policies & procedures.

ASSESS YOUR OWN REVIEW PRACTICES

Exercise #2
Self-Assessment
Reviewing Someone Else's Writing

Instructions:
Each question presents a scenario you might encounter as you review someone else's writing. For each item, circle the one answer that most closely represents what you actually do on the job.

1. You have edited a draft report for conciseness. The report is due to be issued tomorrow, and you feel you have not changed the meaning. Do you?
    A. Insert the revisions and tell the writer to go ahead and issue the report.
    B. Return your revisions to the writer for his or her review and comments.
    C. Meet with the writer and discuss your revisions.

2. A section of a draft report is unclear at first reading, but you are able to identify the message. Do you?
    A. Revise the section to make it more clear.
    B. Ask the writer to describe the message to you and then suggest that the writer revise the section.
    C. Return the section to the writer with your comments and ask the writer to revise it.

3. A draft document does not sufficiently convey the business significance of a project finding. Do you?
    A. Suggest descriptive language the writer might use and ask the writer to incorporate it.
    B. Change the language or content to better describe the significance of the finding.
    C. Ask the writer to explain the significance of the project finding and then coach the writer to revise the draft.

TO REVISE OR NOT TO REVISE

4. You identify and correct several grammatical errors in a report from a staff member whose writing skills are generally good. Do you?
    A. Make the changes and issue the report.
    B. Return your changes to the writer and ask for his or her comments.
    C. Discuss your changes with the writer.

5. A report draft is wordy. The writer has limited experience and needs to improve her writing skills. Do you?
    A. Discuss some examples of wordiness with the writer and then ask her to edit the rest of the document for conciseness.
    B. Edit the draft for conciseness, explain your changes to the writer, and ask for input.
    C. Edit for conciseness, and see that the writer gets a copy of your changes.

6. The tone of a letter is inappropriately strong and you want to soften it. The writer has limited experience writing this type of letter. Do you?
    A. Show the writer where the tone is too strong and ask him or her to revise the wording.
    B. Change the strong words and explain your rationale to the writer.
    C. Suggest word changes and ask the writer what he or she thinks.

7. An experienced writer has submitted a report that does not conform to your department's standards for report format and organization. Do you?
    A. Make the necessary changes and issue the report.
    B. Return the report to the writer, refer to the department's standards, and ask him or her to change it.
    C. Explain the department's report standards to the writer and ask the writer to revise the draft.

ASSESS YOUR OWN REVIEW PRACTICES

8. You are a project leader, and several other individuals will be contributing sections to the report. Before you start composing, do you?
    A. Have each contributor submit a summary so that you can compose the draft report.
    B. Assign the appropriate section to each contributor and ask that the draft be submitted for your review.
    C. Hold a team meeting to discuss the report topics and how to present them in the report.

9. An inexperienced writer is about to write her first report for your review. Do you?
    A. Ask the writer to review prior reports to get a feel for the department's style.
    B. Meet with the writer to discuss standards and expectations for the report.
    C. Ask the writer to read the department's standards on report writing and come to you with any questions.

10. A team member's writing skills are not satisfactory and are not improving. Do you?
    A. Spend more time than usual editing his or her drafts.
    B. Discuss the team member's level of writing skill with him or her and develop a plan for training and improvement.
    C. Send the team member to a writing class.

TO REVISE OR NOT TO REVISE

Exercise #3
Self-Assessment
Reviewing Someone Else's Writing

Instructions:
Circle any and all of the following statements that you feel are representative of your review process.

1. You feel you spend too much time editing other people's writing.

2. You frequently rewrite sections of draft documents.

3. The quality of your work team's writing is not improving.

4. The quality of documents is declining.

5. You repeatedly make the same types of revisions to your team members' writing.

6. Editorial comments are primarily critical.

7. There is little discussion of changes between reviewer and writer.

8. Writers may not review revisions to their drafts before the revisions are finalized.

ASSESS YOUR OWN REVIEW PRACTICES

Notes

TO REVISE OR NOT TO REVISE

Notes

IDENTIFY YOUR LEVEL OF REVIEW

CHAPTER 2

 Identify Your Level of Review

Key Points

- Identify Your Level of Review
- Recognize Multiple Levels of Review
- Identify Four Levels of Review
- Communicate Your Level of Review
- Measure the Payback from Each Level of Review

TO REVISE OR NOT TO REVISE

Notes

CHAPTER 2
Identify Your Level of Review

Identify Your Level of Review

The first question writers often ask is, "What are my bosses looking for when they review my writing?" How would you respond if a team member walked up to you with that question? Why don't you try answering that question right now?

What am I looking for when I review my team members' writing?

_____

_____

_____

_____

_____

_____

_____

_____

_____

_____

_____

_____

TO REVISE OR NOT TO REVISE

Recognize Multiple Levels of Review

The fact is, you are probably looking for a lot of things. As a supervisor or manager responsible for the quality of work done and documents issued, you have multiple interests when you review a document written by a team member. You may want to assess the extent of work performed, judge the appropriateness of conclusions reached, or ensure the accuracy of a report. You may also want to make sure the report is readable, or that it expresses a certain preferred style.

These multiple interests make report review challenging and interesting. At the same time, they can add cost and confusion to an already demanding task.

For many professionals, report review is an intuitive process. Managers explain that they can recognize an effective report when they see it. They can also identify sections of a document that don't sound right, or need revision, and they can often revise drafts to meet their expectations.

The same managers, though, cannot always explain to writers just what they are looking for when they review a draft. They may speak in general terms, saying that they are looking for clarity, completeness, or conciseness. But what is clear to the writer may not be clear to the reviewer. And the writer may have thought she was being concise when the reviewer says she was being incomplete. The dichotomy that reviewers face—knowing what sounds right but not being able to explain it—is a fundamental cause of confusion between writers and editors. Managers may feel frustrated that they have to wait helplessly for a good report to appear.

Managers may feel they cannot put in an order for the perfect report because they cannot define the features they want. Their hope may be that when the ideal report arrives, they will be able to show it to their team members as a model of what they would like to see in the future.

For writers, the ambiguity is equally troubling. Writers want to please their bosses, but they don't know how to do so. They crave direction but don't want rigid rules that stifle their own styles.

To clear up the confusion, writers and reviewers need to be able to talk about the levels at which business documents are typically reviewed. Such discussion must clarify the issue of what reviewers are looking for.

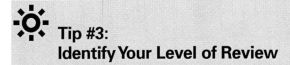

Tip #3: Identify Your Level of Review

An effective reviewer needs to answer the writer's first question:

"What is my boss looking for when he or she reviews my writing?"

Identify Four Levels of Review

Most professionals review documents at one or more of the following levels.

1. **Substance**
2. **Readability**
3. **Correctness**
4. **Style**

Some reviewers focus on one level, while others cover them all. Understanding what happens at each level is critical to building communication between writers and reviewers.

TO REVISE OR NOT TO REVISE

Substance covers the essential meaning and content of a document. It includes elements such as the following.

Appropriateness of content:
- Does the report address the readers' interests and emphasize the most significant points?
- Are the conclusions logical in view of the supporting information?

Completeness and sufficiency of information:
- Does the document present all pertinent data?
- Does it have the right amount of information to support conclusions and to give the reader a full understanding of the subject?

Relevance:
- Does the document target the readers' level of knowledge and interest in the subject matter?
- Does the document accomplish its intended goals?

Tone and balance:
- Are words chosen to convey a tone appropriate to the message and the audience?
- Does the document balance positive and negative aspects of the subject matter?
- Are issues put into perspective?

Readability covers the ease of finding and understanding information. It includes elements such as the following.

Conciseness:
- Are ideas expressed in as few words as possible?
- Does every word count?

Organization:
- Are the most significant issues placed up front?
- Does each section start with a key point?
- Is it easy to find and follow the topics of the document?

IDENTIFY YOUR LEVEL OF REVIEW

Word choice:
- Are words understandable to the intended audience?
- Are words concrete and descriptive?
- Are abbreviations or acronyms explained?

Format:
- Is it easy to find information?
- Is the page layout attractive and easy to read?
- Do headings guide the reader through the document?

Correctness focuses on conformance to established rules and includes the following elements.

Grammar and punctuation:
- Are sentences grammatically correct?
- Are sentences properly punctuated?
- Is capitalization handled correctly?

Consistency:
- Is formatting (including margins, style of headings, and font type and size) consistent throughout the document?
- Are names, terms, and abbreviations presented the same way throughout the document?

Organizational or departmental standards:
- Does the document conform to any particular requirements set by the department or organization?

Style refers to a particular manner of expression and includes the following.

Organizational or departmental conventions:
- Does the document display any particular naming conventions, abbreviations, or word choices that have been established as organizational or departmental style preferences?

Personal preference:
- Does the document conform to the reviewer's personal preferences?

TO REVISE OR NOT TO REVISE

Four Levels of Review

Level of Review	Key Elements
Substance	■ Appropriateness of content ■ Completeness of information ■ Relevance ■ Tone and balance
Readability	■ Conciseness ■ Organization ■ Word choice ■ Format
Correctness	■ Grammar and punctuation ■ Consistency ■ Organizational or departmental standards
Style	■ Organizational or departmental conventions ■ Personal preference

IDENTIFY YOUR LEVEL OF REVIEW

Example of the Levels of Review

there should be *a stronger* focus on training of employees. Training of new employees and periodic updating is important to any organization. Also, cross-training employees could be an asset to the organization, and many employees will appreciate the opportunity to gain a greater understanding of *other* areas. We recommend management perform a comprehensive and fresh look at the training approach. Additionally, training courses should be developed for significant changes in policies *and* procedures.

- **Deleted:** *Based on our review and discussion with various personnel it appears*
- **Deleted:** *an increased*
- **Deleted:** *very*
- **Comment:** *This sentence is ambiguous and seems unnecessary*
- **Comment:** *What is this opinion based on? Is there factual evidence from interviews supporting this idea, or does the sentence reflect your personal opinion?*
- **Deleted:** *around them*
- **Comment:** *It is not possible to "perform" a look. Perhaps you can say "take a look." Also, please consider making the language of this sentence more concrete and action-oriented. Management can "take a look" without making any changes. Just what actions do you recommend to management?*
- **Deleted:** *take this opportunity to*
- **Comment:** *"or seminars" is repetitive of "training courses."*
- **Comment:** *Avoid the passive voice. Be more precise by indicating who should develop training.*
- **Deleted:** *or seminars*
- **Comment:** *Avoid use of symbols in narrative writing*
- **Deleted:** *&*

For each of the editorial changes or comments made, identify the level of review applied.

⊙ **See the CD-ROM for an explanation of the review comments.**

29

TO REVISE OR NOT TO REVISE

Communicate Your Level of Review

Recognizing the four levels of review is the first step in communicating to writers "what you are looking for." You must be objective and candid in identifying the level of review you are actually performing, as confusion about these levels can result in misunderstandings between reviewers and writers.

I have had intriguing responses to a survey I often conduct in workshops I teach on writing and reviewing business reports. In a group of co-workers, consisting of both writers and reviewers, I ask the reviewers to answer this question:

- *At which of the four levels of review do you edit most frequently?*

In the same group, I ask the writers to answer this question:

- *At which of the four levels of review does your boss edit your work most frequently?*

The answers are surprising because they usually differ between the two groups. Reviewers typically say they edit most frequently for substance or readability. Writers typically say their bosses edit most frequently for style. Who is right? And are both parties actually considering the same scenario?

The only way to reconcile differing perceptions is to establish clear communication between writers and reviewers. The remaining chapters of this book will show you how to communicate expectations, explain what you are looking for, and give feedback to writers. Meanwhile, the next section of this chapter considers the immediate payback offered by each level of review.

IDENTIFY YOUR LEVEL OF REVIEW

Exercise #4
Consider Your Review Style

Instructions:
Now that you have read about the four levels of review, think about the editing you usually do and consider the following questions.

1. *At which of the four levels of review do you edit most frequently?*

2. *Do you edit at all four of these levels, or do you skip one or more levels?*

3. *At which of the four levels are you most comfortable editing someone else's writing?*

4. *How do you convey to writers the level of review you are performing?*

Exercise #5
Assess Your Own Levels of Review

Instructions:
Return to the self-assessment exercise you completed on page 14. Review your changes and editorial comments and tally your editorial marks in each category indicated.

How many times did you?

A. Change punctuation, spelling, or grammar _____
B. Change a word or phrase _____
C. Delete a word or phrase _____
D. Rearrange words or information _____
E. Rewrite a phrase or sentence _____
F. Raise a question on the meaning _____

TO REVISE OR NOT TO REVISE

Next, enter the total number you recorded for each type of change listed above.

A	B, D, & E	C	F
Correctness	Style	Readability	Substance

Now, look at the level of review indicated under each letter. This describes the type of editorial change or comment you made.

Note: You may feel that changes you made in categories D and E were for readability rather than style. However, if you did not clearly explain your rationale for the change, the writer is likely to perceive your rewrites as reflecting your personal preference.

Measure the Payback from Each Level of Review

Each of the four levels of review produces results of differing value. While attention to all four levels is necessary to produce a high quality document, you must be judicious in how and when you apply each of these levels.

The cost of reviewing for substance, readability, correctness, or style is the same—your hourly wage multiplied by the time you spend—but the value differs substantially at each level. Reviewing for substance has the potential for creating the greatest value. Honing the conclusions, selecting persuasive and relevant evidence, conveying an appropriate tone—all such review comments can increase the effectiveness of the document.

The next greatest return comes from reviewing for readability, which ensures that the document is attention-getting, easy to read, brief, and descriptive. Reviewing for correctness also adds some value, as accuracy is a reflection of the thoroughness and professionalism of the work done.

The smallest payback comes from reviewing for style. Making language conform to organizational, departmental, or personal preferences may increase the reviewer's comfort level, but it does not have a measurable impact on the effectiveness of a document.

IDENTIFY YOUR LEVEL OF REVIEW

Productive reviewers spend the greatest proportion of their time concentrating on substance, ensuring that the message is appropriate and the supporting evidence is sound. The payback diminishes as reviewers move through the remaining three levels of review.

The Diminishing Returns of the Four Levels of Review

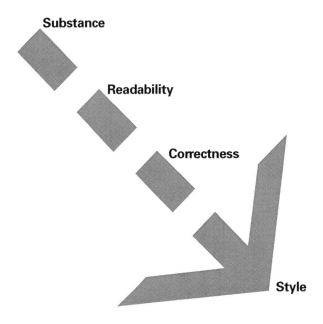

The cost of the review process is measured on the basis of the reviewer's time, not the number of changes made by the reviewer.

The most cost-effective review takes place when:
- **The bulk of the review time focuses on substance.**
- **Review time is limited.**
- **Editorial changes are few.**
- **The quality of the document is high.**

TO REVISE OR NOT TO REVISE

Tip #4:
Identify Your Level of Review

The cost of reviewing for substance, readability, correctness, or style is the same—your hourly wage multiplied by the time you spend—but the value differs substantially at each level. Reviewing for substance has the potential for creating the greatest value.

Tip #5:
Identify Your Level of Review

How do you know if it's personal preference?

If you find yourself thinking, *"I would have said it another way,"* or *"I think it sounds better like this,"* your review comment probably reflects personal preference.

When reviewing for substance or readability, you should be able to explain the reason for your suggested change. E.g., *"To make your point more persuasive, you might give the % of the total value."*

In the following chapters, you will learn how and when to apply each level of review to get the most out of your review time. You will also learn how your understanding of the four levels of review will enable you to make your review process more productive. Knowing how to apply the levels of review will help you to:

- Define your expectations to writers.
- Assess individual writing skills.
- Communicate feedback so that writers improve their writing skills.

IDENTIFY YOUR LEVEL OF REVIEW

Notes

TO REVISE OR NOT TO REVISE

Notes

IDENTIFY AND SELECT YOUR REVIEW STYLE

CHAPTER 3

 Identify and Select Your Review Style

Key Points

- ➢ Recognize Three Review Styles

- ➢ Let the Situation Determine Your Review Style

- ➢ Consider the Effects of Your Review Style

TO REVISE OR NOT TO REVISE

Notes

CHAPTER 3
Identify and Select Your Review Style

Recognize Three Review Styles

How you deliver your review comments to a writer affects the results you get from the review process. Your manner of communicating the desired changes to the writer determines your **Review Style**. I have identified three primary review styles, which I describe below. It is likely that you will recognize all three styles and that you have used all of them at one time or another.

As I describe the styles, I will discuss the pros and cons of each one. Following the descriptions, I will explain the most appropriate uses for each of the three review styles. As you read the descriptions, note what aspects of your own editorial techniques you recognize.

The fist review style is that of **Reviser**. A reviser makes direct changes to the text of a document and may or may not share the changes with the writer before issuing the document. The **Reviser Style** epitomizes what a traditional copy editor does. An editor reviews someone else's text and makes direct corrections and improvements.

The advantages of the **Reviser Style** include the following:

- It is fast.
- It is exact.
- It achieves the precise change desired by the reviewer.

TO REVISE OR NOT TO REVISE

While the **Reviser Style** is quick and effective, it also presents some drawbacks.

The disadvantages are:

- It reflects only one person's point of view.
- It decreases the writer's motivation and pride of authorship.
- It inhibits the writer's ability to learn from the review process.
- The review comments tend to be critical, focusing on the changes to be made.

Another review style is that of **Adviser**. Using this style, a reviewer makes direct changes to the text of a document. In addition to making the changes, the **Adviser** explains the reason for the changes to the writer or asks for the writer's input on the suggested changes.

The advantages of the **Adviser Style** are:

- It achieves the reviewer's desired changes.
- It helps the writer understand the reason for editorial changes.
- It allows for discussion between the writer and the reviewer.
- It helps explain the reviewer's expectations to the writer.

Some disadvantages of the **Adviser Style** include the following:

- It takes more time than revising.
- It emphasizes the reviewer's point of view.
- The reviewer is dictating the changes by making direct revisions to the text.
- The review comments tend to be critical, focusing on the changes to be made.

The third review style is that of **Coach**. A reviewer using the **Coaching Style** does not make direct changes to the text. Instead, the **Coach** provides feedback (both oral and written) that enables the writer to make improvements to his or her own writing. Under this approach, the reviewer provides direction, and the writer makes the revisions.

IDENTIFY AND SELECT YOUR REVIEW STYLE

The benefits of the **Coaching Style** are many:

- It helps teach writers how to write better.
- It encourages discussion and collaboration between reviewers and writers.
- It incorporates the points of view of both the writer and the reviewer.
- It ensures the accuracy of the message delivered in the document.
- The author retains ownership of the document.
- Feedback is balanced, discussing both the positive and negative aspects of the document.

While offering many benefits, the **Coaching Style** also has a cost. Its drawbacks include the following:

- It is time-consuming in its initial stages.
- It requires keen communication and coaching skills on the part of the reviewer.
- The reviewer may not get the exact wording changes that he or she would have liked.
- The writer may be slow to show improvement.

Let the Situation Determine Your Review Style

An effective reviewer uses all three styles discussed above. The key to success is selecting and using the appropriate style for the particular circumstances you are facing. A good editor will not pick one review style and stick to it, because each style accomplishes different goals. A good editor will choose the style appropriate to the situation.

When is the Reviser Style *appropriate?*

Because the **Reviser Style** has a positive effect on the document but a potentially negative effect on the writer, reviewers should limit their use of this style. It is best to reserve the **Reviser Style** for those times when the review feedback would not have an influence on the writer's skill. Revising is often the right choice under the following circumstances.

TO REVISE OR NOT TO REVISE

- The changes focus primarily on correctness.
- There is only one acceptable solution.
- There is no need or desire to improve the writer's skills.

Remember, revising will get the changes made quickly, but it will not result in an improvement in the writer's future documents.

When is the Adviser Style *appropriate*?

Using the **Adviser Style** is often a good first step in training or coaching writers to develop better writing skills. It is most effective under the following circumstances.

- When you are working with inexperienced or unskilled writers who need direction.
- When you work regularly with a writer and need to establish open communication.
- When you want to show the writer that you respect his or her ability to write well and to learn to write even better.
- When editorial comments focus primarily on readability and correctness.

When is the Coaching Style *appropriate*?

The **Coaching Style** may be the most challenging, but it is also the most rewarding in the long run. While it requires additional time up front, that cost will be paid back many times over as writers improve their documents and reviewers spend less time editing. Because it is a time-consuming approach, the **Coaching Style** need not be used all the time, but its payback is great under the following circumstances.

- The writer and reviewer will be working together again on future writing assignments.
- There is a need and a desire to improve the writer's skills.
- There is a need and a desire to build the writer's pride of authorship.
- The writer knows more about the subject matter than the reviewer.

IDENTIFY AND SELECT YOUR REVIEW STYLE

- The writer can benefit from up-front direction from the reviewer.
- Editorial comments are primarily on the substance of the document.

Exercise #6
Identify Your Own Review Style

Instructions:
Return to the self-assessment exercise you completed on pages 15-17 and circle your responses on the following score sheet. Add the number of responses in each column to get a total for each review style.

Item #	Reviser	Adviser	Coach
1	A	B	C
2	A	C	B
3	B	A	C
4	A	B	C
5	C	B	A
6	B	C	A
7	A	B	C
8	A	B	C
9	A	C	B
10	A	C	B
Total			

Effective reviewers need to demonstrate flexibility in their choice of review style. Consider how your profile looks on this scoring sheet.

Continue to another score sheet on the next pages for further interpretation of your responses.

TO REVISE OR NOT TO REVISE

Exercise #7
Identify Your Own Review Style

Instructions:
Using the self-assessment exercise you completed on pages 15-17, compare your response to each item to the suggested answers below.

Item #	Suggested Response	Suggested Review Style
1	B	Adviser
2	B	Coach
3	C	Coach
4	A	Reviser
5	A	Coach
6	C	Adviser
7	B	Adviser
8	C	Coach
9	B	Coach
10	B	Coach

Tally the total number of your responses that match the suggested answers above. _____

Effective reviewers must select a review style deliberately so that it is appropriate to the situation.

⊙ **See the CD-ROM for an explanation of the suggested answers.**

IDENTIFY AND SELECT YOUR REVIEW STYLE

Select the Appropriate Review Style for the Situation

Review Style	Use This Style When:
Reviser	■ The changes focus primarily on correctness. ■ There is only one acceptable solution. ■ There is no need or desire to improve the writer's skills.
Adviser	■ You are working with inexperienced or unskilled writers who need direction. ■ You work regularly with a writer and need to establish open communication. ■ You want to show the writer that you respect his or her ability to write well and to learn to write even better. ■ Editorial comments focus primarily on readability and correctness.
Coach	■ The writer and reviewer will be working together again on future writing assignments. ■ There is a need and a desire to improve the writer's skills. ■ There is a need and a desire to build the writer's pride of authorship. ■ The writer knows more about the subject matter than the reviewer. ■ The writer can benefit from up-front direction from the reviewer. ■ Editorial comments are primarily on the substance of the document.

TO REVISE OR NOT TO REVISE

Three Styles of Review

Review Style	Characteristics
Reviser	■ Makes direct changes to the text. ■ May or may not explain changes to the writer.
Adviser	■ Makes direct changes to the text. ■ Explains reasons for the changes or asks for input from the writer.
Coach	■ Provides direction and feedback enabling the writer to improve his or her document.

⊙ *See the CD-ROM for examples of how each Review Style might communicate with a writer.*

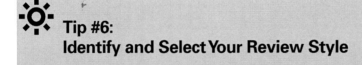

Tip #6:
Identify and Select Your Review Style

An effective reviewer needs flexibility to choose the appropriate review style (Reviser, Adviser, or Coach).

However, the choice should not be arbitrary. The review style should fit the circumstances and be chosen for its positive effect on the writer's ability to learn.

IDENTIFY AND SELECT YOUR REVIEW STYLE

 **Tip #7:
Identify and Select Your Review Style**

Consider the following when choosing your Review Style:

- Nature of the working relationship between writer and reviewer

- Level of review performed

- Skill level of the writer

- Degree of flexibility allowed in the document

Do not let time constraints dictate your choice of review style. A tight deadline is no excuse to revert to the **Reviser Style.**

Consider the Effects of Your Review Style

Your choice of review style affects one thing and one thing only: the writer's ability to learn from the review process. If there is no need for the writer to learn, the **Reviser Style** is likely to be the quickest and most cost-effective review style. However, using **Reviser** as a dominant review style guarantees that the reviewer will continue to spend a lot of time editing other people's writing.

For copy editors whose job is to ensure the correctness and accuracy of documents, the **Reviser Style** may be appropriate and acceptable to the writer. After all, the editor is the expert on language, grammar, and punctuation. Most writers are happy to benefit from the copy editor's expertise.

Still, copy editors must remember that the **Reviser Style** is best confined to editing for correctness. If editing spills over into substance and style, then the copy editor should take full advantage of the benefits offered by the **Adviser** and **Coach** styles.

TO REVISE OR NOT TO REVISE

If you are a business manager or professional who would like to spend less time editing, you will find much opportunity in being an **Adviser** and a **Coach** to your writing team. You will increase the effectiveness of documents by encouraging writers to consider issues of substance over issues of style. You will contribute to your colleagues' training and skill-building by showing them how to improve their writing. Finally, you will build morale and motivation among the professionals who need to write documents for your review.

IDENTIFY AND SELECT YOUR REVIEW STYLE

Notes

TO REVISE OR NOT TO REVISE

Notes

CHAPTER 4

Build a Double-Payback Review Process

Key Points

- Measure the Return from Your Editing Time

- Calculate the Cost of a Single-Purpose Review

- Review Drafts at the Appropriate Level

- Select the Most Effective Review Style for the Circumstances

TO REVISE OR NOT TO REVISE

Notes

CHAPTER 4
Build a Double-Payback Review Process

Measure the Return from Your Editing Time

The time you spend reviewing someone else's writing is costly. Therefore, you want to get as much payback as possible from that time. Most writers and reviewers see payback in the form of improvements to the document being reviewed. This indeed is the first and most visible result from the time spent editing and reviewing. However, that payback is usually not big enough to result in a net profit from the time spent editing.

To get the greatest profit from your review time, you need to build a double-payback process that accomplishes two goals simultaneously.

1. **Improve the effectiveness of the current document.**

2. **Improve the writer's ability to write better documents in the future.**

If you are simply improving the current document, your editorial time is a direct and continuing cost. If you focus on improving the writer's future skills, your editorial time is an investment that will produce ongoing returns.

TO REVISE OR NOT TO REVISE

The Effect of the Review Process on Current and Future Documents

BUILD A DOUBLE-PAYBACK REVIEW PROCESS

My experience is that most managers use a single-purpose approach to reviewing others' writing. Their focus is on getting a document done and delivered, and they may not think much about the effect of their editing on future documents. The reality is that your editing does have an effect on future documents, whether you realize it or not. The reason for this is that writers respond to the review process in one way or another. They may do any of the following.

1. Writers may ignore review feedback and simply let the manager make any changes he or she desires. This response will result in no change to future documents the writer composes. The writer will simply continue writing the same way.

2. The writer may respond positively to review feedback. In this case, the writer may accept changes, seek to understand their purpose, and apply what he or she has learned to the next document.

3. The writer may respond negatively to review feedback. The author may become defensive or discouraged and may produce an even worse document the next time around, expecting that the manager will revise it anyway.

Rather than letting anything happen, a productive reviewer can guide the writer's response by using the following practices for a double-payback review process.

1. **Calculate the cost of a single-purpose review.**
2. **Review drafts at the appropriate level.**
3. **Select the most effective review style for the circumstances.**

TO REVISE OR NOT TO REVISE

Calculate the Cost of a Single-Purpose Review

It is ironic that business managers use the **Reviser Style** so often, for this creates a single-purpose review practice. As the writer has no opportunity to learn from the **Reviser**, the effect of the editing is solely on the current document. This results in a continuing cost with little opportunity for future improvement.

It is also curious that managers are so often willing to redo the work of their team members by using the **Reviser Style**. It is only in the realm of writing that managers seem willing to step in and actually redo the work of their team members.

Now let's consider your usual review practices by assessing your responses to the self-assessment exercise on page 18. If you checked off three or more items on that list, it is likely you are using a single-purpose review practice. All the items on the list are symptomatic of a single-minded review that focuses primarily on the report being reviewed, not on the skills of the writer.

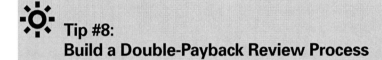

Tip #8:
Build a Double-Payback Review Process

Follow these five steps to build a double-payback review process.

1. Calculate the cost of a single-purpose review.
2. Review drafts at the appropriate level.
3. Select the most effective review style for the circumstances.
4. Coach authors to improve their writing skills.
5. Build pride of authorship.

BUILD A DOUBLE-PAYBACK REVIEW PROCESS

Review Drafts at the Appropriate Level

If you edit every draft you receive at each of the four levels (substance, readability, correctness, and style), you may be unknowingly perpetuating a single-purpose review. Why? Writers may feel discouraged by so much revising, and they may give up trying to write better documents. "It will be changed anyway," writers have been heard to say, "so I won't bother fine tuning this document. My boss will edit it as he or she sees fit."

Still, you may feel it is your responsibility to review a document thoroughly each time you see it. So how can you be comfortable and at the same time avoid over-editing? You can do this by recognizing where you are in the review process and acting accordingly.

If you are reviewing a document once and only once, then it is perfectly fine to cover all four levels in your review. However, if you are reviewing a document several times, there is no need to duplicate your work with each review. In fact, to get the most out of your review time, you should limit yourself to two passes through most documents.

The first review should be primarily for substance. If you are satisfied with the substance at first reading, you can immediately complete your editing by continuing to review for readability and correctness. If you have comments or questions on substantive issues, you should consult with the writer to resolve those first. After you are satisfied with the substance of the document, you can review it a second time for readability and correctness.

If you are one of multiple reviewers of the same document, choosing your level of review is even more important. Imagine having three editors and all three editors going at the document on all four levels. The author might feel overwhelmed at getting so many review comments or revisions. And what if the three editors offer differing editorial comments? The writer is likely to be confused or even frustrated.

TO REVISE OR NOT TO REVISE

Review First for Substance

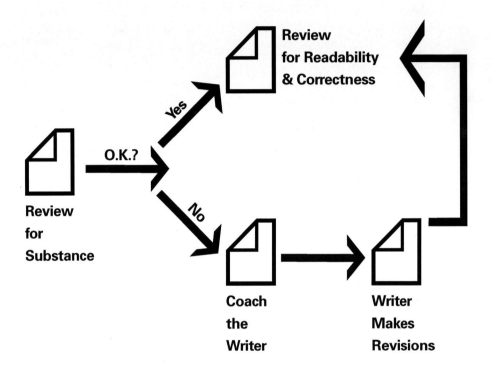

BUILD A DOUBLE-PAYBACK REVIEW PROCESS

Sample Review Responsibilities For Multiple Reviewers

Reviewer	Primary Reviewer for:
Team Leader	Substance
Technical Editor	Readability Correctness
Reviewer	**Secondary Reviewer for:**
Manager	Substance Readability
Director	Substance

The **primary reviewer** is accountable for the quality of the document at the level indicated.

The **secondary reviewer** is responsible for approving the work of the writer and primary reviewer and makes additional suggestions or changes only when he or she determines that the document does not meet the work team's standard for publication.

TO REVISE OR NOT TO REVISE

Multiple reviewers need to coordinate their editing approach. Each reviewer should have a primary review responsibility based on his or her position in the editorial chain. While there may be a small amount of overlap among the reviewers, each one should rely on the work of the previous reviewer and not duplicate his or her work.

One reviewer may be assigned as the primary editor responsible for the quality of the document at all levels. In that case, the additional reviewers would do only two things: 1) offer substantive comments reflecting his or her knowledge and point of view, and 2) correct any obvious errors missed by the previous reviewer.

In other cases, the reviewers may divide the responsibilities. The first reviewer may focus primarily on substance while another concentrates on readability and correctness. Alternatively, it may be the other way around.

Select the Most Effective Review Style for the Circumstances

As described in the previous chapter, each review style (Reviser, Adviser, or Coach) affects the writer's ability to learn. Therefore, the **Adviser** and **Coaching** styles are more amenable to a double-payback review. The more you communicate and share expectations with writers, the more learning that takes place.

Familiarize yourself with the appropriate uses of each review style as described on page 45. When you start revising a document because it seems like the most expedient thing to do, consider whether the author might learn something from your advice or coaching.

Tip #9: Build a Double-Payback Review Process

The Benefits and Risks of the Review Process

Reviewing someone else's writing can result in two tangible **benefits**:

- A better document
- Better documents from the writer in the future

Reviewing someone else's writing also presents **risks**.
As a reviewer, you may:

- Change the meaning inadvertently.
- Enforce your personal style without being aware of it.
- Discourage the writer by over-editing.
- Forget to give positive feedback to reinforce good writing.
- Delay issuance of the document.
- Add cost that is not outweighed by the value added by the editorial changes.

The following chapters will discuss techniques for coaching writers and building pride of authorship—two techniques that will greatly expand the value of your review time.

TO REVISE OR NOT TO REVISE

Notes

COACH WRITERS TO WRITE BETTER

CHAPTER 5

Coach Writers to Write Better (And Maybe Even Want to Write More)

Key Points

- Learn from Experience
- Talk to Your Team Members
- Give Clear Direction to Writers
- Use Guidelines and Templates to Coach Writers
- Give Constructive Feedback to Writers
- Use a Coaching Discussion to Resolve Issues of Substance
- Contribute to Your Team's Training in Writing Skills
- Assess the Cause of Continued Writing Problems

TO REVISE OR NOT TO REVISE

Notes

CHAPTER 5
Coach Writers to Write Better (And Maybe Even Want to Write More)

Learn from Experience

In my early days as an editor in the business world, I did not do much coaching. My job title actually was "editor," and so I felt justified revising my colleagues' work. I often spent hours on a document. The most challenging cases were those in which the message of the document simply was not clear. Other difficult cases had either too much or too little information to meet the readers' needs.

In such challenging cases, I prided myself on being able to figure out what the writer was trying to say and then saying it for him. I could take a garbled paragraph and make a coherent point out of it. I could take a page worth of data and boil it down to two or three key numbers. The rewriting was difficult, but also rewarding.

One day, I received a report that was so confusing, I went straight over to the author's desk and asked her to explain it to me. As she talked, I started to understand her key points. In fact, she described the issues so much more clearly in her oral comments than she had in her written report. After listening to her, I said, "What you just told me is really clear. Why don't you write that up?" "Okay," she responded, "but I don't remember the exact words I used to explain it to you. It will take a lot of work to rewrite it."

TO REVISE OR NOT TO REVISE

I learned two valuable lessons from that experience. First, I was amazed to find out that the writer did know what she meant to say, even though she had not said it in writing. It turned out that I didn't have to figure out what she was trying to say—she could explain it to me. Second, I learned that if I was going to ask authors to revise their own work, I needed to develop a new set of skills. It wasn't enough to say, "Okay, now rewrite your report." The writer did not feel—justifiably—that she had enough skill or experience to do a quick rewrite.

This experience led me to transition from being a **Reviser** to being a **Coach**, and I have had much more free time ever since. I no longer spend hours reconstructing incoherent paragraphs. I no longer feel I am reading through code and translating it into understandable language. But the greatest value came not from the reduction in my editing time, but rather from the improvement in writers' skills. It was dramatic. It did not, however, happen overnight. I had to learn how to be a **Coach**. Now, with many years of experience, I will share the process I developed and practiced to become an effective writing coach.

Tip #10:
How to Coach Writers to Write Better

Talk to your work team about their writing. As a coach, you cannot pass the players notes or play the game for them. You can establish face-to-face communication.

- Give clear direction to writers.
- Offer constructive feedback.
- Use a coaching discussion to resolve issues of substance.
- Contribute to the team's training.

COACH WRITERS TO WRITE BETTER

Talk to Your Team Players

Face-to-face communication is a crucial component of an effective review process. Coaches cannot simply pass notes to players on their performance, and they cannot run out onto the field and play the game for them. The coach's job is to enable the players to play the game the right way. And that is precisely your job as a business manager who reviews other people's writing. Like the athletic coach, you guide your team by giving instructions, observing, and offering feedback and direction.

Give Clear Direction to Writers

In a sincere effort to encourage creativity and ownership, managers often instruct team members to write a document in whatever form and style they see fit. This is a fantastic approach if in fact the manager is willing to accept any form and style the writers may come up with. In many cases, however, this free-form approach backfires when the reviewer receives the draft and starts revising it.

Most organizations and departments have some pre-determined criteria for the documents they produce. If you have such criteria, writers need to know them up front so that they can meet them. If you do not have defined criteria for standard documents your team produces, perhaps you should. You need to communicate objective criteria to writers if you want to help them improve their writing skills.

To get the best document possible from a writer, you must communicate your expectations before a writer composes a first draft. While you want to allow room for flexibility, you must also communicate any boundaries to that flexibility. This saves time, eliminating any guessing games or false starts. It also avoids the frustration writers feel when they receive criticisms that could have been avoided with some prior input.

The elements you should communicate before writers write are described on page 69.

TO REVISE OR NOT TO REVISE

If you have an established work team and documented criteria for the deliverables produced, you will not need to communicate these issues for every writing assignment. What is important to determine is whether each team member knows what your expectations are for the items listed.

When a new member joins your team, it is imperative that you communicate expectations before he or she starts writing.

The level of detail you provide in giving direction to writers will depend on your answers to the following questions.

- Do you have an established format for the documents your team writes?
- Are there specific requirements for the substance of the documents your team writes?
- Are writers writing documents for somebody else's signature rather than their own?

If the answer is "Yes" to the three questions above, your direction to writers will need to be detailed and explicit. You may benefit from providing written guidance, as I describe in the next section.

> "Quality is conformance to requirements.... People perform to the standards of their leaders."
>
> — Philip B. Crosby, *Quality Is Free*

COACH WRITERS TO WRITE BETTER

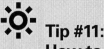
Tip #11:
How to Coach Writers to Write Better

Give clear direction to writers. Communicate the following expectations before a writer composes a first draft.

- Criteria for content and substance of the document.
- Departmental or organizational format and style.
- Standard writing references used by your work team.
- Due dates for draft and final reports.
- Your preferred review process.

Use Guidelines and Templates to Coach Writers

Helpful tools for providing up-front direction to writers include writers' guidelines or document templates. Written guidelines describe specific expectations for content and readability. Templates establish a fixed format and may also include guidelines or tips on substance and readability.

Tip #12:
How to Coach Writers to Write Better

Use writers' guidelines and templates to provide direction to writers.

Writers' guidelines should be specific to the type of document writers produce. They should focus on the substance of the document.

Templates outline a consistent format for a particular type of document. They take the guess work out of decisions on page layout, font, and organization of the document.

 See the CD-ROM enclosed with this book to see samples of writers' guidelines and document templates.

TO REVISE OR NOT TO REVISE

Give Constructive Feedback to Writers

As a coach, you will be giving regular feedback to your writers. Before you read the following section, take a few moments now to complete the following checklist.

Which of the following represent effective feedback to a writer? Circle any and all items that are effective.

1. "I like this sentence."
2. "Use the active voice."
3. "Unclear. Please revise."
4. "Good report."
5. "What is the effect of this point?"
6. "Poor organization."
7. "You can be more concise by deleting the words I circled."
8. "Weak example."
9. "Please quantify the estimated cost rather than calling it 'minimal.'"
10. "Wordy."

To be constructive, the feedback you give writers should be:

- **Objective**
- **Specific**
- **Helpful**

Objective feedback is based on established criteria. It uses language known to both the writer and reviewer, and it represents standards that have been previously communicated to writers. Let's take an example. Item #2 above, *"Use the active voice,"* is objective feedback in that it is based on criteria described in many books on grammar and style. However, it is effective if and only if the writer and reviewer have the same understanding of what the active voice is, and if the reasons for and against the active voice have been discussed with the writer.

Similarly, Item #9 is objective provided that the work team has discussed and agreed that quantification is a desired element in their written deliverables.

In contrast, subjective feedback may represent personal preference, and it is nearly impossible for a writer to act on. For instance, Item #6, *"Poor organization,"* and Item #8, *"Weak example,"* seem to express the reviewer's opinion. Even worse, the writer would be hard pressed to act on the feedback, because the reviewer has not indicated what aspect of the organization is unacceptable or what is wrong with the example used.

Tip #13:
How to Coach Writers to Write Better

Avoid the following types of feedback that writers cannot learn from or act on.

- Judgments

- Generalizations

- Comments delivered after the fact

Specific feedback points out a particular aspect of a defined piece of text. Item #7 in the list above is an example of specific feedback. The reviewer has highlighted specific text to comment on and has also communicated an objective criterion—the need to be concise.

Generalizations, such as Item #10, *"Wordy,"* do not provide much direction to the writer. Even Item #4, *"Good report,"* may not be helpful to the writer in the long run. All the writer knows is that something pleased the reviewer, but he does not know what aspects of his writing caused this positive response.

TO REVISE OR NOT TO REVISE

Helpful feedback is something the writer can act on and learn from. Subjective comments and generalizations are not helpful, as discussed above. Feedback must also be delivered at the right time in order to be helpful. Remember that you must communicate established criteria before the writer composes a first draft, not after it is all written. You should also deliver your feedback sufficiently in advance of any due date so that the writer can both accept and apply the comments.

Tip #14:
How to Coach Writers to Write Better

Writers need feedback from the review process to learn to improve their writing skills.

Constructive Feedback is:

Nature of the Feedback	Key Characteristics
Objective	■ Based on established criteria. ■ Represents standards that have been previously communicated to writers.
Specific	■ Points out a particular aspect of a defined piece of text.
Helpful	■ The writer can act on and learn from it.

Use a Coaching Discussion to Resolve Issues of Substance

If you are confused by the text of a draft, or if you feel content should be added or removed, you have probably identified an issue of substance and should use a coaching discussion to resolve the issue with the writer. While you may address feedback relating to readability or correctness by using the **Adviser** or **Reviser** styles, issues of substance demand a coaching discussion.

A coaching discussion will accomplish two goals:

- It will ensure the accuracy of the revised document.
- It will help the writer learn.

To be successful, coaching must be done skillfully. Just talking to a writer or giving oral feedback may not constitute effective coaching. To be a good coach, you need to be able to do the following.

- Use objective criteria in delivering your feedback to writers.
- Explain the reason for your change, suggestion, or question.
- Communicate feedback in a nonjudgmental way.
- Avoid generalizations.
- Ask pertinent questions regarding the substance of the document.
- Listen attentively.
- Acknowledge when the author is right.
- Offer balanced feedback, both positive and negative.
- Support the writer's efforts to improve.
- Avoid personal preference.
- Refrain from rewriting.

Remember that the coach's goal is to enable the writer to write it right the next time. You should always be asking yourself, "How can my feedback help the writer?"

TO REVISE OR NOT TO REVISE

On the next page, I describe the coaching process I use frequently with writers. It takes some work the first time or two with a writer, but after that, get ready to go to the beach, as you won't have much editing to do.

 **Tip #15:
How to Coach Writers to Write Better**

Use a **coaching discussion** to resolve issues of substance.

An effective coaching session will achieve the following two paybacks:

- Ensure the accuracy of the revised document.

- Help the writer learn to write better documents in the future.

Angela's Coaching Process

I go through the following steps when I set out to review the substance of a document.

- Read the document for substance, taking note (on a separate sheet of paper) of questions and suggestions I have.

- Add notes on the positive aspects of the document.

- Talk with the writer (either face-to-face or by phone) and do the following:
  - ✔ Deliver positive feedback.
  - ✔ Ask questions on the substance.
  - ✔ Listen to the writer's responses and take notes of what might be used in the revised text.
  - ✔ Make my suggestions for possible revisions, giving the reasons based on objective criteria.

- Ask the writer to revise the document based on our discussion. Confirm that he or she has sufficient understanding to improve the document. If necessary, recap any notes I took from our discussion.

- Review the revised document and give feedback to the writer.

TO REVISE OR NOT TO REVISE

What happens if the author's revision is not good enough? This is a troubling consideration to many managers, and it is enough to stop some of them from trying to coach writers.

Some managers have told me that they have a coaching discussion with the writer, read the second draft, and then proceed to revising the document as they see fit. In this case, the coaching discussion has lost its value. To be a good coach, you have to be willing to accept what is acceptable and refrain from "perfecting" the document or imposing your personal preference—even if that is just a few wording changes.

Certainly, you may need to make some necessary revisions after the author produces a second draft. These should be limited to correcting obvious mistakes in grammar, spelling, or punctuation and making minor suggestions for improving readability.

If the author's revision is far below your expectations, you need to assess the cause of the performance problem.

- Was your coaching sufficiently objective, specific, and supportive to help the writer understand the desired improvements?
- Have you given clear direction on specific requirements for the type of document the writer is composing?
- Did the writer listen, respond, and collaborate during the coaching process?
- What is the level of the writer's core skills in composition, readability, and correctness? Does he or she need additional training?

Remember that, as you are asking writers to improve their skills, you are also improving your skills as a coach. Practice. Ask writers how helpful your feedback was. Try something new the next time you coach. Keep track of effective techniques that work with your team. Give positive feedback to writers to encourage them.

COACH WRITERS TO WRITE BETTER

Tip #16:
How to Coach Writers to Write Better

What happens after a coaching discussion?

- If the writer produces an acceptable revision, give positive feedback on the improvement.

- If the revision is not acceptable, explore the cause of the problem.

  ✔ Was the coaching sufficiently objective, specific, and supportive?

  ✔ Were clear directions provided to the writer?

  ✔ Did the writer listen, respond, and collaborate?

  ✔ What is the level of the writer's core skills?

Remember that coaching is part of a skill-building process.

Contribute to Your Team's Training in Writing Skills

I get many calls from managers asking me to come to their organizations and put on a training program to teach their staff to write better. Early in my career, I accepted some of these invitations at face value and delivered the requested training. Invariably in these cases, the participants would voice a complaint to me early in the training. "My boss is the one who needs to be here," they would say. "We're just trying to write reports the way he wants them." Some writers

TO REVISE OR NOT TO REVISE

would even say, "My drafts are fine. When my boss edits them, she makes them wordy and ambiguous. I don't think she improves my writing at all. She's the one who needs training."

These writers were right. Their bosses did need to be there. But it wasn't necessarily because their bosses didn't know how to write. It was because their bosses didn't know how to coach the writers. The bosses' biggest mistake was to spend money and time on training the staff without taking the following critical preliminary steps.

How to Offer Writing Training That Works

If you feel that training would benefit your entire team, it is best to conduct an in-house session that all members attend. Before you schedule such a session, be sure you have selected tarining that meets certain criteria. The training must be:

- Targeted to the type of documents your work team produces.
- Customized to convey your specific expectations for written deliverables.
- Based on objective criteria and skills inventories that are relevant to your types of documents.
- Hands-on, allowing participants the opportunity to apply what they learn.
- Team-oriented, encouraging writers and reviewers to work together as they should on the job.
- Results-oriented, culminating in measurable action plans for the group and for individuals.

Talk directly to the instructor you are considering. Share sample documents with the instructor well in advance of the training. Review detailed course descriptions to select skill-building that your team needs. You do not need to spend large amounts of time or money to get the kind of program that will work for you. You do, though, need to be confident that the instructor will teach skills that are in accordance with your expectations.

COACH WRITERS TO WRITE BETTER

Tip #17:
How to Coach Writers to Write Better

If skill-building is necessary, offer training that will get the results you want. Be sure the training is:

- Targeted to your team's type of documents.
- Customized to your expectations.
- Based on objective criteria.
- Hands-on.
- Team-oriented.
- Results-oriented.

When it comes time for the in-house workshop, make sure your entire team participates. That includes you and any other people who edit your team's writing. Working together, the team members will learn to share consistent criteria for their writing, to understand each other's roles and perspectives, and to communicate expectations and feedback to one another in a constructive manner.

If skill-building is needed by just one or a few individuals in your work team, you will need to play an active role in their development. Don't just send someone to a writing workshop and expect that to work miracles. It may help, but how do you know the workshop will teach the right things?

Here is what you can do to make sure individual training meets your goals:

- Work with the individual(s) to identify specific strengths and weaknesses in writing skills.
- Make sure any weaknesses identified relate to the individual's writing skills and not to the lack or insufficiency of established criteria for the types of documents produced.

- Select resources (workshop or self-study) that target the weaknesses identified. You or the individual(s) may do the research to find appropriate sources of training.
- Set goals for the individual's participation in the training.
- Following the training, give balanced feedback on the writer's progress. Coach the individual to encourage continued skill-building.

Tip #18:
How to Coach Writers to Write Better

To raise the quality level of documents your team produces and to cut editing time dramatically, maintain a regular skill-building process.

- Define expectations and objective criteria for the documents your team produces.
- Communicate the expectations to all team members.
- Develop reviewers' coaching skills.
- Develop individual's writing skills.
- Give balanced feedback to writers.
- Periodically assess the team's writing and review practices.

Assess the Cause of Continued Writing Problems

If you find that poor writing is a continuing problem among your work team, or if you observe that professionals are frustrated and demoralized over their writing assignments, you may need to look beyond the surface to identify the cause.

COACH WRITERS TO WRITE BETTER

Problems that surface in written documents may be symptomatic of problems elsewhere in the work process. Here are some of the issues I have identified as I have worked with groups of professionals to solve writing problems:

- Insufficient level or quality of work done.
- Inconsistent or incomplete criteria for the documents being produced.
- Time constraints or unclear priorities for managing time.
- Lack of ownership or accountability for the quality and timeliness of documents.
- Insufficient understanding of the readers' needs.

Training someone how to organize a document, how to write more concisely, or how to punctuate correctly will not solve any of these problems. In these cases, training would be a waste of time and money. As a manager responsible for the documents written by your work team, you have the obligation to assess all causes of writing problems and provide resources to help professionals achieve the desired standards.

Tip #19:
How to Coach Writers to Write Better

Three ingredients are critical to successful writing and review.

1. Clear criteria communicated to writers.

2. Competency in writing skills among writers and reviewers.

3. Constructive review process and feedback to writers.

A work team must have all three elements in place if they are to produce high-quality, timely documents.

TO REVISE OR NOT TO REVISE

Notes

BUILD PRIDE OF AUTHORSHIP

CHAPTER 6

 Build Pride of Authorship

Key Points

- Establish Ownership

- Be Sensitive to Writers' Sensitivities

- Establish Two-Way Communication

TO REVISE OR NOT TO REVISE

Notes

CHAPTER 6
Build Pride of Authorship

Establish Ownership

A writer in one of my recent workshops made the following comment: "What you are seeing is not representative of my writing. This is really my boss's report." "But your name is on the report," I responded. "That doesn't mean anything," I heard in reply. "My boss edits everything I write, and I just let him say it the way he wants. It's not my report."

I have heard similar comments frequently. Such thoughts raise the questions, "Whose report is it anyway? And does it matter?" I believe strongly that the perceived ownership of the document does indeed matter, as it has a profound impact on both the quality and the cost of the document. Furthermore, ownership is important because someone has to catapult the document through to its publication.

Too many business documents end up as orphans when they begin passing through the review process. They become less desirable than a hot potato, with ownership shifting from one person to another and no one wanting to take final possession.

Every document needs an owner—both in name and in spirit. Writing is hard work, and only those writers who feel their pride of authorship will work hard enough to write well.

TO REVISE OR NOT TO REVISE

You must carefully consider where ownership of a document should lie. If someone else is writing for your signature, you may in fact be the owner of the document even though you do not write it. In this case, you may feel free to take more liberties in editing, even applying your personal preferences. After all, it is your name on the document. Still, if you want the person writing for you to do his or her very best job, it would be wise to build as much ownership as possible on the part of the writer.

If you are reviewing documents that you are approving but that carry the writer's signature, then it would be wise to let the writer be the owner.

Tip #20:
How to Build Pride of Authorship

The perceived ownership of a document matters, as it has a profound impact on both the quality and the cost of the document.

Every document needs an owner—both in name and in spirit. Writing is hard work, and only those writers who feel their pride of authorship will work hard enough to write well.

Be Sensitive to Writers' Sensitivities

A group of 15 professionals recently shared memories of their early days in the business world. Most of them told sad tales of feeling chagrined, embarrassed, angered, or discouraged. They were all talking about their first experience with having their writing edited by someone else!

Writers are some of the most sensitive creatures on earth, and crossing out a writer's words may be like crossing paths with a skunk. He'll raise a stink and put up defenses to keep you away.

BUILD PRIDE OF AUTHORSHIP

Defensiveness closes the door to communication and collaboration. If you want to help a writer improve, you have to minimize the likelihood of a defensive reaction. You can do this by paying attention to the details.

> **"Did you ever know a writer to just take a piece of criticism and shut up?"**
>
> **— F. Scott Fitzgerald, in a letter to H.L. Menken**

Lose the red pen.
Nothing makes a writer see red more quickly than your red pen. If you are editing on hardcopy, use blue or green ink—softer colors that are less jarring when they land on the writer's desk. If you are using the "Track Changes" function in Word, you can change the color of your editorial marks by going to Tools—Options—Track Changes—Color.

Make most review notes on a separate page.
To a writer, the most crushing experience is to see a page of his or her work covered with changes and editorial marks. It looks like something retrieved from a battleground.

Start with positive feedback.
Sure, it's easy to criticize, but where were you when the writer struggled over every word of the first draft? Don't start right out with your criticisms. Begin by acknowledging the many things done well by the writer.

Ask, don't assume.
In 99 percent of the cases, the writer knows more about the subject matter than you do. The document, after all, represents his or her work product. When you have doubts about the meaning, tone, or word choice, ask the writer. Don't assume you know what the writer is trying to say and then say it for her.

TO REVISE OR NOT TO REVISE

Suggest, don't dictate.
Every time I hear a reviewer say, "I changed this word to that word," or "I took out that sentence," I cringe. It sounds so dictatorial. What is the writer to do but simply let the reviewer make the change (and then relinquish ownership). Try suggesting changes, and let the writer consider them.

Let the author be the author.
If you really want to be the wordsmith, you should probably just write the document yourself in the first place. Leave intact as much of the author's original language as possible, and refrain from rewriting.

Let go of personal preference.
Enforcing your style will cause the writer to shut down and give up. If the writer perceives that you are editing for personal preference, he will likely feel that the document is yours once you edit it.

Don't over-edit.
You will never create the perfect document anyway. Know when a document reaches an acceptable level of quality, and let it go.

Respect due dates and deliver your feedback promptly.
Don't be a bottleneck in the process. Be aware of the time line for a document and let the writer know when you will complete your review. Try to turn documents around within 24 hours of receiving them.

Deliver your feedback directly to the writer.
If a team has created the document you are reviewing, talk to the primary author, not necessarily to the team leader. Also try whenever possible to deliver your feedback face-to-face, not through e-mail.

BUILD PRIDE OF AUTHORSHIP

Tip #21: Build Pride of Authorship

Be sensitive to writers' sensitivities to reduce defensiveness and establish open communication.

- Lose the red pen.
- Make most review notes on a separate page.
- Start with positive feedback.
- Ask, don't assume.
- Suggest, don't dictate.
- Let the author be the author.
- Let go of personal preference.
- Don't over-edit.
- Respect due dates and deliver feedback to the writer promptly.
- Deliver feedback directly to the writer.

Establish Two-Way Communication

Reviewers and editors often communicate in one direction—they tell things to the writer. If the writer is to retain authorship, though, the review process needs to be a two-way street. Writers and reviewers need to see each other coming and going, and they need to meet in the middle to discuss where they've been and what's ahead.

You can establish two-way communication with writers by remembering to do the following.

Be available to advise.
Don't wait until the writer has done all the work and then start talking about the document. Give guidance up front, and let writers know you are available to answer questions as they compose their drafts.

TO REVISE OR NOT TO REVISE

Listen to and be willing to accept the writer's point of view.
Sometimes the writer is right. You may at first reading think a word change is desirable, but then the writer may explain to you why that word is meaningful to the reader. Acknowledge legitimate reasoning, and be willing to yield to the author when appropriate.

Ask for feedback on your own writing.
Put yourself in the writer's shoes occasionally. It will remind you how it feels to be edited by someone else. It also gives your team members a chance to turn the tables. Most important, it helps writers and reviewers practice working together.

Candidly assess your own writing strengths and weaknesses.
Are you really a better writer than all your team members? Hold yourself to a high standard and be sure that you have mastered the mechanics of good business writing.

Find, use, and share helpful resources such as grammar books and style guides.
References are useful tools for both writers and reviewers. Have on hand a few books that you can use to answer questions as they arise. Don't horde writing books on your own desk—get copies for your team members as well.

Develop your coaching skills.
Good coaching takes practice. If you are not comfortable coaching writers, you should take advantage of books, workshops, or mentors that can help you develop your communication and feedback skills.

BUILD PRIDE OF AUTHORSHIP

Tip #22:
Build Pride of Authorship

Establish two-way communication between reviewers and writers so that they can work together to create the best document. As a reviewer, you can:

- Be available to advise.
- Listen to the writer's point of view.
- Ask for feedback on your own writing.
- Assess your own writing skills.
- Use and share resources such as grammar books and style guides.
- Develop your coaching skills.

TO REVISE OR NOT TO REVISE

Commitments for Producing High Quality, Timely Documents

The Reviewer's Commitments

I Will:

- Establish and communicate expectations for the documents my work team produces.

- Use objective criteria for reviewing other people's writing.

- Avoid applying personal preference.

- Use Advising and Coaching to help writers improve their skills.

- Give feedback that is objective, specific, helpful, and timely.

- Be sensitive to writers' sensitivities and refrain from rewriting.

- Recognize that no one writes perfectly and there is no such thing as the perfect document.

- Remember that it is easy to criticize but much harder to write it right yourself.

- Master the mechanics of good writing and correct grammar.

BUILD PRIDE OF AUTHORSHIP

Commitments for Producing High Quality, Timely Documents

The Writer's Commitments

I Will:

- Write the best draft I can.

- Ask for direction when I am uncertain what my boss expects in a document.

- Use the writing resources my organization or work team makes available.

- Accept review feedback in the spirit of learning.

- Do self-review and proofreading before I turn the document over to someone else.

- Respond promptly to the reviewer's feedback.

- Ask for explanation of any editorial comment I don't understand.

- Speak up if a reviewer has changed my meaning.

- Be able to explain why I wrote something the way I did.

- Master the mechanics of good writing and correct grammar.

TO REVISE OR NOT TO REVISE

Is Peer Review for You?

Peer review can sometimes lessen the editing done by a manager or supervisor. It can also take the sting out of professionals having their writing revised by their bosses. To be successful, though, it must be done right.

Peer Review Can Work Well When:

- Established criteria exist for the documents the work team creates.
- Team members have complementary writing skills.
- Team members know how to give constructive feedback.
- Peer reviewers are clear on the level of review they are doing and refrain from applying personal preference.
- Peer review is done expeditiously and before the document is presented to a superior for review.

Peer Review Does Not Work Well When:

- The peer reviewer's writing skills are worse than those of the writer.
- The reviewer is afraid of offending a peer.
- Personal preference comes into play.
- The peer reviewer is not clear on what he or she is looking for.
- Objective criteria do not exist for reviewing documents.

BUILD PRIDE OF AUTHORSHIP

Notes

TO REVISE OR NOT TO REVISE

Notes

CHAPTER 7

Become a Writing Coach: The Game Plan

Key Points

- Stop Editing and Start Coaching
- Build Your Toolkit
- Reap the Rewards of Coaching

TO REVISE OR NOT TO REVISE

Notes

CHAPTER 7
Become a Writing Coach: The Game Plan

Stop Editing and Start Coaching

So you want to stop editing and start coaching writers? Don't be fooled into thinking it will be an overnight transition. You will need to build new skills, practice, and be patient. At first, it may feel you are not saving any time at all, and you may be tempted to revert back to the comfortable Reviser Style. I assure you, though, that the reward will be well worth the investment you make in developing your Coaching skills.

You have already completed the first step: learning about the effects of your review style and discovering alternatives to editing other people's writing. You are ready to start applying your new review techniques with the very next document someone gives you to read.

Build Your Toolkit

As you build your coaching skills, you will find it helpful to gather or develop tools to help you communicate with writers. These tools include the following.

Writers' guidelines: These should be specific to the type of document your work team produces and should focus on substance and readability (including a required or preferred format).

> "Where were you fellows when the paper was blank?"
>
> — Fred Allen, comedian, said to writers who heavily edited his script

TO REVISE OR NOT TO REVISE

Document templates: These should set up the content, format, and page layout for specific documents.

Sample documents: You can select a few samples of final documents for writers to review.

Grammar reference: You should have on hand a standard reference book for issues of grammar and punctuation.

Style guide: Ideally, the style guide should be specific to your organization or department. A style guide establishes consistency by indicating how to handle such things as abbreviations, titles, numbers, etc.

⊙ ***The CD-ROM enclosed with this book offers sample writers' guidelines and templates.***

In addition to the tangible tools mentioned above, you will also need to develop a set of personal skills enabling you to be an effective coach. These include the following.

- Clear and consistent communication
- Constructive feedback
- Active listening
- Encouragement
- Problem-solving
- Writing skills: substance, readability, and correctness

If you want to learn more about coaching skills, I recommend the book ***Coaching for Improved Work Performance*** by Ferdinand F. Fournies (New York: McGraw-Hill, Revised edition, 1999).

Tip #23: Build Your Coaching Toolkit

You will need the following tools to help you be an effective Coach.

Hard Tools
- Writers' guidelines
- Document templates
- Grammar reference
- Style guide

Soft Skills
- Clear and consistent communication
- Constructive feedback
- Active listening
- Encouragement
- Problem-solving
- Writing skills: substance, readability, and correctness

Reap the Rewards of Coaching

As you start doing less revising and start doing more coaching, you will experience many changes in your role as an editor or reviewer. You may initially feel a loss of control; you may even find it uncomfortable to give up your role as a Reviser. If you see the transition through, though, and become an effective Coach, you may find yourself trying to work your way out of an editing job altogether.

Learning to coach writers effectively will help you build a new set of skills that you can apply to all aspects of your work. You will become not just a more effective reviewer, but a more effective manager as well.

TO REVISE OR NOT TO REVISE

You will feel the reward of seeing someone else's skills improve as a result of your input and feedback. You may feel that you have learned to be a good teacher as well as a good manager. You will share in the benefits of writers' increased pride of authorship. Writers will be likely to write more and write better when they feel they are accountable for and retain ownership of the documents they write.

Many of the rewards you will achieve are tangible and measurable, such as the following.

- Less time and cost spent on editing and rewriting.
- Fewer bottlenecks and more timely publication of documents.
- Higher quality of first drafts.

Finally, frustration will diminish among both writers and reviewers. And that alone may make it all worthwhile.

PERSONAL ACTION PLAN

Personal Action Plan

List techniques you will apply in reviewing other people's writing. Reference the page or chapter number so that you can find resources easily.

TO REVISE OR NOT TO REVISE

Personal Action Plan

ABOUT THE AUTHOR

Angela J. Maniak is a leading expert in helping business and government professionals communicate clearly, quickly, and convincingly. Since 1986, Angela has consulted to over 100 organizations and trained thousands of professionals to gain attention, acceptance, and action through their reports and presentations. She has taught throughout the United States and in Africa, Asia, Canada, Europe, Mexico, and South America.

Angela's other published books include:

- ***Tell It to the CEO:*** How to Write Compelling Executive Summaries and Briefings
- ***Writing High-Impact Reports:*** Proven Practices for Auditors and Accountants
- ***Report Writing for Internal Auditors***

Angela has pioneered scores of practical approaches to solving on-the-job writing problems. She has helped her clients slash their writing and review time by 50 percent or more, publish documents on time and at a low cost, and design documents that executives actually read and remember! Angela's approach is practical and to the point. Angela doesn't just advise you on what to do—she shows you precisely how to do it.

www.angelamaniak.com

TO REVISE OR NOT TO REVISE

ORDER FORM

Skill-Builders Press Order Form

SAN: 256-2618

Ship to:

Name: _____ Title: _____

Organization: _____

Shipping Address: _____

City: _____ State/Province: _____ Zip/Mail Code: _____

Country: _____

Phone: _____ Fax: _____

E-mail: _____

Take a discount on quantity purchases! You can mix and match titles.
10-25 copies: 10% discount
26-50 copies: 15% discount
50 + copies: 25% discount

Title	Quantity	Price Ea.	Discount	Total
Writing High-Impact Reports: Proven Practices for Auditors and Accountants		$59.00		
Tell It to the CEO: How to Write Compelling Executive Summaries and Briefings		$59.00		
To Revise or Not to Revise: The Essential Guide to Reviewing Somebody Else's Writing		$49.00		

Please see reverse to continue with your order....

TO REVISE OR NOT TO REVISE

Please add shipping charge of 10% of order price:_____
(Customers outside the U.S., add 20%)

Total submitted: $_____

All payments due in U.S. dollars.
☐ Check enclosed, made payable to Skill-Builders Press
☐ Charge credit card:

Card #_____ Expiration Date_____

Name on Card_____

Type of Card   ☐ Visa   ☐ MasterCard   ☐ American Express

Order Now!
Call: 207-338-0108
Fax: 207-338-0662
Mail: Angela Maniak
           Skill-Builders Press
           191 Prescott Hill Road
           Northport, ME 04849, USA

Want to learn more?
Workshops and consultations are also available. For more information, or to order workbooks, please contact:
   Angela J. Maniak
   207-338-0108
   www.angelamaniak.com